Winning ETF

Learn how to earn money by investing in ETFs to increase your capital and create real income.

Aran Shiren

I0416428

1.Introduction

Exchange-Traded Funds (ETFs) have become increasingly popular in recent years as a way for investors to diversify their portfolios and capitalize on the performance of a wide range of assets. In this article, we will provide an introduction to ETFs, including what they are, how they work, and the benefits and drawbacks of investing in them.

What are ETFs?

ETFs are investment funds that are traded on stock exchanges, similar to individual stocks. They are designed to track the performance of a specific index, commodity, or asset class. ETFs are typically managed by investment companies, which create and redeem shares of the fund based on investor demand.

ETFs can provide investors with exposure to a

wide range of assets, such as stocks, bonds, commodities, and currencies. This diversification can help reduce risk and volatility in a portfolio, as ETFs offer exposure to multiple assets with a single investment.

How do ETFs work?

ETFs are structured as open-ended funds, which means that the number of shares outstanding can change based on investor demand. This allows ETFs to trade on stock exchanges throughout the day, unlike mutual funds, which are priced at the end of each trading day.

When an investor buys shares of an ETF, they are essentially buying a stake in the underlying assets held by the fund. For example, if an ETF tracks the S&P 500 index, the fund will hold a basket of stocks that mirror the performance of the index. As the value of the underlying assets changes, so too will the value of the ETF shares.

Benefits of investing in ETFs

There are several benefits to investing in ETFs, including:

Diversification: ETFs offer exposure to a wide range of assets, which can help mitigate risk and volatility in a portfolio.

Liquidity: ETFs trade on stock exchanges, making them easy to buy and sell throughout the trading day.

Low costs: ETFs typically have lower fees than actively managed mutual funds, which can help investors save money on expenses.

Tax efficiency: ETFs are structured to minimize capital gains distributions, which can help investors reduce their tax liabilities.

Transparency: ETFs disclose their holdings on a daily basis, providing investors with a clear picture of the fund's underlying assets.

Drawbacks of investing in ETFs

While ETFs offer many benefits, there are also some drawbacks to consider, including:

Tracking error: ETFs may not perfectly track the performance of their underlying index, leading to potential discrepancies in returns.

Commissions: Investors may incur trading commissions when buying and selling ETFs, which can eat into their returns.

Lack of control: ETF investors do not have a say in the selection of underlying assets, as the fund is managed by an investment company.

Leveraged and inverse ETFs: These types of ETFs use complex investment strategies to amplify returns or provide inverse exposure to an index, which can increase risk and volatility.

ETFs are a versatile and cost-effective investment vehicle that can provide investors with diversified exposure to a wide range of assets. By understanding how ETFs work and weighing the benefits and drawbacks, investors can make informed decisions about incorporating ETFs into their portfolios.

2.Advantages and disadvantages of ETFs

Exchange-Traded Funds (ETFs) have become increasingly popular investment vehicles in recent years due to their convenience and diversity. ETFs are a type of investment fund that can be traded on stock exchanges much like individual stocks. They offer many advantages, but also come with some disadvantages. In this article, we will explore the various benefits and drawbacks of ETF investing.

One of the main advantages of ETFs is their low cost. Unlike mutual funds, which often come with high expense ratios and management fees, ETFs typically have lower fees because they are passively managed. This means that they track an index, such as the S&P 500, rather than having a team of managers actively selecting and trading securities. As a result, investors can save money on fees and potentially earn higher returns over the long term.

Another advantage of ETFs is their liquidity. Because they trade on stock exchanges, ETFs can be bought and sold throughout the trading day at market price. This makes it easy for investors to enter and exit positions quickly, unlike mutual funds which are only priced at the end of the trading day. Additionally, ETFs can be sold short or bought on margin, providing investors with more flexibility in their trading strategies.

ETFs also offer diversification benefits. By investing in an ETF that tracks a broad index, investors can gain exposure to a wide range of securities across different sectors and industries. This can help reduce risk and volatility in their portfolio, as losses in one sector may be offset by gains in another. ETFs also provide access to asset classes that may be difficult to invest in directly, such as commodities or international stocks.

Furthermore, ETFs are tax-efficient investment vehicles. Because of their structure, ETFs typically have lower capital gains distributions compared to mutual funds. This can help investors minimize their tax liability and maximize their after-tax returns. Additionally, investors can use ETFs to implement tax-loss harvesting strategies by selling ETFs at a loss to offset capital gains in other investments.

On the other hand, there are some drawbacks to investing in ETFs. One potential disadvantage is trading costs. While ETFs have low expense ratios, investors may incur brokerage commissions when buying and selling ETFs. Frequent trading can eat into returns, especially for small investors with limited capital. To mitigate this risk, investors should consider using commission-free ETF trading platforms offered by some brokers.

Another drawback of ETFs is tracking error. While most ETFs are designed to closely track their underlying index, there may be instances where the ETF's performance deviates from the index due to factors such as trading costs, rebalancing, or liquidity issues. This can affect the overall return of the ETF and may lead to underperformance compared to the index it tracks. Investors should carefully review the tracking error of an ETF before investing to ensure it meets their performance expectations.

Additionally, ETFs may lack customization compared to individual stocks or actively managed funds. Because ETFs track an index, investors have limited control over the securities held within the fund. This can be a disadvantage for investors who prefer to customize their portfolio based on specific investment objectives or risk preferences. For those seeking more tailored investment solutions, individual stocks or actively managed funds may be a better fit.

ETFs offer many advantages for investors seeking low-cost, diversified, and tax-efficient investment options. They provide liquidity, diversification, and convenience, making them an attractive choice for both retail and institutional investors. However, investors should be aware of the potential drawbacks, such as trading costs, tracking error, and limited customization. By carefully evaluating the advantages and disadvantages of ETF investing, investors can make informed decisions to build a well-balanced and efficient investment portfolio.

3. Differences between ETFs and mutual funds

ETFs (Exchange-Traded Funds) and mutual funds are two very common and popular investment tools among investors. Both offer investors the opportunity to diversify their portfolio and profit from financial markets, but they have significant differences that are important to know in order to make informed and conscious investment decisions.

In this article, we will analyze the main differences between ETFs and mutual funds, in order to help investors better understand two different but complementary financial instruments.

1. Structure and Management

One of the main differences between ETFs and mutual funds concerns their structure and management method. ETFs are funds that replicate the performance of a benchmark index, such as the S&P 500 or the FTSE MIB. These funds are traded on the stock exchange like stocks and the trading price of an ETF is determined by the real-time market. ETFs are managed passively, meaning they seek to replicate the performance of the benchmark index without making active investment choices.

On the other hand, mutual funds are actively managed by a team of professional managers who make investment decisions in order to achieve the highest returns for investors. Mutual funds consist of a portfolio of selected securities actively managed by the fund managers, who seek to discover investment opportunities and outperform the market in the long term. Mutual funds are not traded on the stock exchange and their price is calculated once a day, at market close.

2. Fees and Costs

Another significant difference between ETFs and mutual funds concerns the fees and costs associated with each instrument. ETFs tend to have lower fees compared to mutual funds, as they are managed passively and do not require continuous management activity by a team of managers. ETF fees are usually expressed in terms of TER (Total Expense Ratio) and are generally lower than mutual funds.

On the other hand, mutual funds tend to have higher fees compared to ETFs, as they are actively managed and require continuous commitment from managers to identify investment opportunities and outperform the market. Mutual fund fees may vary depending on the type of fund and the management policy adopted.

Furthermore, mutual funds may involve additional costs, such as entry and exit fees, management fees, performance fees, and other costs associated with portfolio management. Investors must take into account all costs and fees associated with a fund before deciding to invest in it.

3. Liquidity and Transparency

Another difference between ETFs and mutual funds concerns the liquidity and transparency of the instruments. ETFs are traded on the stock exchange like stocks and are therefore characterized by greater liquidity compared to mutual funds. Investors can buy and sell ETFs at any time during the trading session, obtaining a real-time market price.

On the other hand, mutual funds are not traded on the stock exchange and the liquidity of investments depends on the fund's redemption policies. Usually, mutual funds allow investors to buy and sell fund shares at a price calculated once a day, at market close. This trading method may involve delays in completing buy and sell operations, reducing investment liquidity and flexibility.

Furthermore, ETFs are characterized by greater transparency compared to mutual funds. ETFs replicate the performance of a benchmark index and the holdings that make up the fund's portfolio are publicly available. Investors can check the portfolio composition of an ETF at any time and verify which securities are included in the fund. This transparency allows investors to better assess the risk and profitability of an ETF and understand exactly what they are investing in.

4. Diversification and Market Access

Another important difference between ETFs and mutual funds concerns diversification and access to financial markets. ETFs offer investors a wide diversification through investment in a portfolio of securities that replicate a benchmark index. ETFs allow investors to access global financial markets and invest in different asset classes, sectors, and geographical regions with a single instrument. Investing in an ETF can therefore offer a wide portfolio diversification and risk reduction.

On the other hand, mutual funds offer investors the opportunity to access a wider range of investment strategies and investment opportunities compared to ETFs. Mutual fund managers can select and actively manage a portfolio of securities in order to achieve returns superior to the market. Mutual funds can invest in a variety of assets, such as stocks, bonds, commodities, currencies, and other financial instruments, offering investors the opportunity to diversify their portfolio and invest in a targeted manner based on their needs and investment objectives.

ETFs and mutual funds are two different investment tools that offer investors the opportunity to diversify their portfolio and profit from financial markets. Investors must carefully evaluate the characteristics of each instrument, including structure, management, fees, liquidity, transparency, diversification, and market access, in order to make informed and conscious investment decisions. Both instruments can be used complementarily within a diversified portfolio, allowing investors to benefit from the peculiarities and advantages of each instrument.

4. How do ETFs work?

ETFs, or exchange-traded funds, have become increasingly popular investment options for both individual and institutional investors. But how exactly do they work? In this article, we will explore the mechanics behind ETFs, their advantages, and some key considerations for investors looking to add them to their portfolios.

ETFs are investment funds that are traded on stock exchanges, just like individual stocks. They are designed to track the performance of a specific index, commodity, or basket of assets. This makes them a convenient way for investors to gain exposure to a diversified portfolio of securities without having to buy each asset individually.

One of the key features of ETFs is their low costs. Because they are passively managed, ETFs typically have lower expense ratios compared to actively managed mutual funds. This means that investors can benefit from broad market exposure without incurring high management fees. Additionally, ETFs are generally more tax-efficient than mutual funds, as they have lower turnover rates and do not distribute capital gains as frequently.

Another advantage of ETFs is their liquidity. Since they are traded on stock exchanges, investors can buy and sell ETF shares throughout the trading day at market prices. This provides investors with the flexibility to adjust their portfolios quickly in response to changing market conditions. Additionally, the ability to trade ETFs intraday can help investors implement more sophisticated trading strategies, such as short selling or using options.

ETFs also offer a high degree of transparency. Unlike mutual funds, which are only required to disclose their holdings on a quarterly basis, ETFs generally provide daily updates on their underlying assets. This allows investors to know exactly what they are investing in and make informed decisions about their portfolios.

There are several different types of ETFs available to investors, each with its own unique characteristics. Broad market ETFs, such as those that track major stock indices like the S&P 500, provide exposure to a diverse range of companies across various industries. Sector ETFs focus on specific industry sectors, such as technology or healthcare, allowing investors to target their investments in particular areas of the market. Bond ETFs track the performance of fixed-income securities, providing investors with exposure to the bond market.

In addition to traditional ETFs, there are also leveraged and inverse ETFs. Leveraged ETFs aim to amplify the returns of a specific index or asset class, typically by using derivatives or other financial instruments. Inverse ETFs, on the other hand, seek to profit from the decline of a particular index or asset class. While these types of ETFs can offer increased potential returns for investors, they also come with higher risks and are not suitable for all investors.

When considering investing in ETFs, there are a few important factors to keep in mind. First, investors should carefully research the underlying assets of an ETF to ensure that it aligns with their investment goals and risk tolerance. Additionally, it is crucial to understand the costs associated with ETFs, including expense ratios, trading commissions, and potential taxes.

It is also important to consider the liquidity of an ETF. While most ETFs are highly liquid, some niche or thinly traded ETFs may have wider bid-ask spreads and lower trading volumes, which can impact the ability to buy and sell shares at desirable prices. Investors should pay attention to these factors when selecting ETFs for their portfolios.

Overall, ETFs can be a valuable addition to a well-diversified investment portfolio. They offer investors a cost-effective and transparent way to gain exposure to a wide range of assets, while providing liquidity and flexibility in trading. By understanding how ETFs work and conducting thorough research, investors can make informed decisions about incorporating these investment vehicles into their portfolios.

5.Stock ETFs

ETFs, or exchange-traded funds, have become increasingly popular investment vehicles in recent years. With a wide range of options available to investors, one area that has garnered significant attention is equity ETFs. These types of ETFs provide investors with exposure to the stock market through a diversified portfolio of stocks in one convenient investment.

Equity ETFs are a type of fund that holds a diversified collection of stocks representing a particular segment of the market, such as technology, healthcare, or consumer goods. By investing in an equity ETF, investors are able to gain exposure to a specific sector or industry without having to purchase individual stocks.

One of the key benefits of investing in equity ETFs is diversification. By holding a basket of stocks, investors are less exposed to the risks associated with owning individual stocks. This diversification can help to mitigate the impact of poor performing stocks in the ETF, as gains in other stocks within the fund can help offset any losses.

Another advantage of equity ETFs is their low cost. Compared to actively managed mutual funds, which typically have higher fees and expenses, equity ETFs tend to have lower expense ratios. This means that investors can achieve similar market exposure at a lower cost by investing in an equity ETF.

Furthermore, equity ETFs are traded on major stock exchanges, just like individual stocks. This means that investors can buy and sell shares of an equity ETF throughout the trading day at market prices. This added liquidity and flexibility make equity ETFs a convenient and easy way to invest in the stock market.

One of the most popular equity ETFs is the SPDR S&P 500 ETF Trust (SPY). This ETF tracks the performance of the S&P 500 index, which is made up of 500 of the largest publicly traded companies in the United States. By investing in SPY, investors can gain exposure to the broader U.S. stock market and benefit from the growth potential of some of the largest and most well-known companies in the country.

For investors looking to gain exposure to specific sectors or industries, there are a wide variety of equity ETFs available. For example, the Technology Select Sector SPDR Fund (XLK) provides exposure to the technology sector, while the Consumer Staples Select Sector SPDR Fund (XLP) focuses on consumer staples companies. By choosing ETFs that align with their investment goals and risk tolerance, investors can construct a diversified portfolio tailored to their needs.

In addition to sector-specific ETFs, there are

also thematic ETFs that focus on specific investment themes or trends. For example, the Global X Robotics & Artificial Intelligence ETF (BOTZ) invests in companies that are leading the way in robotics and artificial intelligence technology. Thematic ETFs allow investors to capitalize on emerging trends and industries that have the potential for strong growth.

When considering investing in equity ETFs, it is important for investors to conduct thorough research and due diligence. This includes understanding the underlying holdings of the ETF, the fund's performance history, and the fees and expenses associated with investing in the fund. Investors should also consider their investment goals, risk tolerance, and time horizon when selecting equity ETFs for their portfolio.

Overall, equity ETFs can be a valuable tool for investors looking to gain exposure to the stock market in a diversified and cost-effective manner. With a wide range of options available, investors have the opportunity to tailor their investment strategy to align with their financial goals and risk tolerance. By investing in equity ETFs, investors can access the potential for equity market returns while benefiting from the convenience and flexibility of an exchange-traded fund.

6.Bond ETFs

ETFs, or exchange-traded funds, have gained increasing popularity among investors in recent years due to their lower costs, diversification benefits, and ease of trading. While most investors are familiar with equity ETFs, the bond ETF market has also seen significant growth. Bond ETFs, also known as fixed-income ETFs, offer investors exposure to a wide range of bonds, including government, corporate, and municipal bonds. In this article, we will focus specifically on bond ETFs, exploring what they are, how they work, and their advantages for investors.

What are Bond ETFs?

Bond ETFs are investment funds that are traded on stock exchanges and hold a portfolio of bonds. These ETFs can track a specific bond index or be actively managed by a team of investment professionals. Bond ETFs provide investors with access to a diversified portfolio of bonds without having to purchase individual bonds themselves. This diversification can help reduce risk by spreading exposure across different issuers, sectors, and maturities.

How do Bond ETFs Work?

Bond ETFs work similarly to equity ETFs in that they are liquid, transparent, and trade in real-time on stock exchanges. When investors buy shares of a bond ETF, they are essentially buying a piece of the fund's portfolio. The value of the ETF is based on the value of the underlying bonds it holds. Bond ETFs also pay interest, or coupon payments, to investors at regular intervals, just like individual bonds.

Advantages of Bond ETFs

There are several advantages to investing in

bond ETFs. One key advantage is the diversification they offer. By holding a variety of bonds in one fund, investors can spread risk and reduce the impact of any single bond defaulting. Bond ETFs can also provide exposure to different sectors and credit qualities, allowing investors to customize their bond portfolios based on their risk tolerance and investment objectives.

Another advantage of bond ETFs is their liquidity. Since they trade on stock exchanges, bond ETFs can be bought and sold throughout the trading day at market prices. This liquidity gives investors the flexibility to adjust their bond allocations quickly and efficiently, unlike individual bonds that may be less liquid and more difficult to trade.

Additionally, bond ETFs typically have lower costs than actively managed bond funds. Since bond ETFs are passively managed and track an index, they have lower expense ratios and fewer management fees compared to actively managed funds. Lower costs can translate into higher returns for investors over the long term.

Types of Bond ETFs

There are several types of bond ETFs available to investors, each with its own investment objective and risk profile. Some common types of bond ETFs include:

- Government Bond ETFs: These ETFs invest in bonds issued by government entities, such as U.S. Treasury bonds or government agency bonds. Government bonds are generally considered to be low-risk investments, as they are backed by the full faith and credit of the government.

- Corporate Bond ETFs: These ETFs invest in bonds issued by corporations. Corporate bonds typically offer higher yields than government bonds but also come with higher credit risk. Corporate bond ETFs can be further divided by credit quality, ranging from investment-grade to high-yield bonds.

- Municipal Bond ETFs: These ETFs invest in bonds issued by state and local governments. Municipal bonds offer tax advantages for investors, as the interest income is usually exempt from federal taxes. Municipal bond ETFs can provide investors with exposure to a stable and tax-efficient source of income.

- High-Yield Bond ETFs: These ETFs invest in bonds with lower credit ratings, typically rated below investment grade. High-yield bonds offer higher yields to compensate for higher credit risk. High-yield bond ETFs can be appealing to income-seeking investors looking for higher returns.

Risks of Bond ETFs

While bond ETFs offer many benefits to investors, they also come with risks that investors need to understand. One key risk is interest rate risk. Bond prices are inversely correlated with interest rates, meaning that when interest rates rise, bond prices fall. Since bond ETFs hold a portfolio of bonds with varying maturities, they are subject to interest rate risk. Investors in bond ETFs may experience losses if interest rates rise unexpectedly.

Another risk of bond ETFs is credit risk. Bond ETFs that invest in lower-quality bonds or high-yield bonds are exposed to the risk of issuer default. If a bond issuer fails to make interest or principal payments, it can lead to losses for investors in the ETF. Credit risk is higher in high-yield bond ETFs compared to investment-grade bond ETFs.

Finally, liquidity risk is a concern for bond ETF investors. While bond ETFs are generally liquid investments, there may be instances where trading volumes are low or market conditions are unfavorable, leading to wider bid-ask spreads and potential price discrepancies. Investors should be aware of liquidity risks when trading bond ETFs, especially during times of market stress.

Bond ETFs can be a valuable addition to a diversified investment portfolio, offering investors exposure to a broad range of bonds in a cost-effective and efficient manner. By providing diversification, liquidity, and lower costs, bond ETFs can help investors achieve their investment goals while managing risks effectively. However, investors should carefully consider the risks associated with bond ETFs, such as interest rate risk, credit risk, and liquidity risk, before investing. Consulting with a financial advisor can help investors determine the most suitable bond ETFs for their individual investment needs and risk tolerance.

7. Sector ETFs

Exchange-Traded Funds (ETFs) have become increasingly popular investment vehicles in recent years, providing investors with a convenient way to gain exposure to a diverse range of asset classes. Among the various types of ETFs available, "sector ETFs" have gained attention for their ability to target specific industries or sectors of the economy. In this article, we will explore the concept of sector ETFs, how they work, their benefits and risks, and considerations for investors looking to include them in their portfolios.

What are sector ETFs?

Sector ETFs are a type of exchange-traded fund that focuses on a specific sector of the economy, such as technology, healthcare, energy, or consumer staples. These ETFs are designed to track the performance of a specific sector index, providing investors with exposure to companies operating within that sector. By investing in a sector ETF, investors can gain diversified exposure to a particular industry without having to pick individual stocks.

How do sector ETFs work?

Sector ETFs work similarly to other types of ETFs, in that they are listed and traded on stock exchanges like individual stocks. The ETFs hold a portfolio of securities that represent the companies within a specific sector, with the goal of tracking the performance of a sector index. The ETFs may use various strategies, such as capitalization-weighting or equal-weighting, to determine the composition of the portfolio.

Investors can buy and sell shares of sector ETFs throughout the trading day, providing them with liquidity and flexibility in managing their investments. Sector ETFs also offer the benefits of diversification, as they typically hold a basket of stocks within the sector, reducing individual company risk.

Benefits of sector ETFs

Sector ETFs offer several benefits for investors looking to gain exposure to specific industries or sectors of the economy. Some of the key advantages of sector ETFs include:

1. Diversification: Sector ETFs provide investors with exposure to a diversified portfolio of companies within a particular sector, reducing individual company risk.

2. Ease of access: Sector ETFs are traded on stock exchanges, making them easily accessible for investors to buy and sell throughout the trading day.

3. Cost-effective: Sector ETFs often have lower expense ratios compared to mutual funds, making them a cost-effective way to gain exposure to specific sectors.

4. Flexibility: Sector ETFs allow investors to focus on specific industries or sectors of the economy, providing them with the flexibility to tailor their investment portfolios to their preferences.

5. Performance potential: Sector ETFs can offer investors the potential for enhanced performance if a particular sector experiences strong growth or outperforms the broader market.

Risks of sector ETFs

While sector ETFs offer several benefits, it is important for investors to be aware of the risks associated with investing in these funds. Some of the key risks of sector ETFs include:

1. Sector concentration risk: Sector ETFs are focused on a specific sector of the economy, which can lead to concentration risk if that sector underperforms or experiences a downturn.

2. Market risk: Like all investments, sector ETFs are subject to market risk, including fluctuations in the broader market that can impact the performance of the fund.

3. Economic and political risk: Sector ETFs can be affected by economic and political factors that impact the specific sector they are focused on, such as changes in government regulations or economic conditions.

4. Liquidity risk: While sector ETFs are traded on stock exchanges, they may have less liquidity than broad-based ETFs, which can

impact the ease of buying and selling shares.

Considerations for investors

Before investing in sector ETFs, investors should consider several factors to determine if these funds are suitable for their investment objectives and risk tolerance. Some key considerations include:

1. Investment goals: Investors should evaluate their investment goals and objectives to determine if investing in sector ETFs aligns with their overall investment strategy.

2. Risk tolerance: Sector ETFs can be more volatile than broad-based ETFs, so investors should assess their risk tolerance and ability to withstand potential fluctuations in a specific sector.

3. Portfolio diversification: Investors should consider how sector ETFs fit within their overall investment portfolio and ensure they are properly diversified across various asset classes.

4. Sector outlook: Investors should assess the outlook for the specific sector they are considering investing in, including factors such as industry trends, competition, and regulatory environment.

5. Expense ratios and fees: Investors should compare the expense ratios and fees of sector ETFs to ensure they are getting a cost-effective investment option.

In conclusion, sector ETFs can be a valuable tool for investors looking to gain exposure to specific industries or sectors of the economy. These funds offer diversification, ease of access, and potential for enhanced performance, but also come with risks that investors should be mindful of. By carefully evaluating their investment goals, risk tolerance, and the characteristics of sector ETFs, investors can make informed decisions about whether to include these funds in their portfolios.

8.Geographic ETFs

Geographic ETFs, also known as geographically focused exchange-traded funds, are investment instruments that allow investors to allocate their assets to specific regions or countries around the world. These ETFs are designed to track the performance of a particular geographic area, providing investors with exposure to companies within that region. In recent years, the popularity of geographic ETFs has grown significantly as investors look for ways to diversify their portfolios and capitalize on opportunities in different parts of the world.

One of the key advantages of geographic ETFs is their ability to provide investors with exposure to a specific region or country without having to invest directly in individual stocks. This can be particularly beneficial for investors who are looking to diversify their portfolios and reduce their overall risk exposure. By investing in a geographic ETF, investors can gain exposure to a broad range of companies within a specific region, which can help to reduce the impact of individual stock performance on their portfolio.

In addition to providing investors with exposure to specific regions or countries, geographic ETFs also offer investors the opportunity to benefit from the growth potential of emerging markets. Emerging markets are often considered to be more volatile than developed markets, but they also offer the potential for higher returns. By investing in a geographic ETF that focuses on emerging markets, investors can gain exposure to these markets while also benefiting from the diversification and risk management features of an ETF.

Another advantage of geographic ETFs is their ability to provide investors with exposure to sectors or industries that may be concentrated in a specific region. For example, a geographic ETF that focuses on technology companies in Asia may provide investors with exposure to some of the largest and fastest-growing technology companies in the world. By investing in this ETF, investors can gain exposure to these companies without having to invest directly in individual stocks, which can be time-consuming and risky.

One of the challenges of investing in geographic ETFs is that they can be subject to currency risk. Since these ETFs are often denominated in a foreign currency, changes in exchange rates can impact the value of the ETF. For example, if an investor buys a European ETF denominated in euros and the euro weakens against the U.S. dollar, the value of the ETF may decrease even if the underlying stocks are performing well. To mitigate this risk, investors can hedge their exposure to foreign currencies by investing in currency-hedged ETFs or using other hedging strategies.

When considering investing in geographic

ETFs, investors should carefully evaluate the investment objectives, underlying assets, and performance history of the ETF. They should also consider the fees associated with the ETF, as well as any tax implications of investing in foreign securities. Additionally, investors should be aware of the risks associated with investing in specific regions or countries, such as political instability, regulatory changes, and economic downturns.

Overall, geographic ETFs can be a valuable tool for investors looking to diversify their portfolios and gain exposure to specific regions or countries. By carefully evaluating the risks and potential rewards of investing in geographic ETFs, investors can make informed decisions that align with their investment objectives and risk tolerance. With the increasing availability of geographic ETFs on the market, investors have more options than ever to capitalize on opportunities around the world and build a well-diversified investment portfolio.

9. Smart beta ETF

Smart beta ETFs combine the benefits of both passive and active investing strategies. While traditional market-cap weighted ETFs passively track an index, smart beta ETFs use a rules-based methodology to provide exposure to factors such as value, growth, momentum, low volatility, and quality. These factors are designed to outperform the broad market over the long term by exploiting market inefficiencies and investor biases.

There are several key characteristics of smart beta ETFs that differentiate them from traditional ETFs. First, smart beta ETFs offer investors exposure to specific factors or investment themes that may not be available in market-cap weighted ETFs. For example, an investor looking to tilt their portfolio towards high-quality stocks may choose a smart beta ETF that tracks an index of high-quality companies.

Second, smart beta ETFs offer the potential for outperformance compared to traditional market-cap weighted ETFs. By focusing on factors that have been shown to drive returns over time, such as value or momentum, smart beta ETFs seek to deliver superior risk-adjusted returns. This can be particularly attractive for investors looking to enhance the performance of their portfolios without taking on excessive risk.

Third, smart beta ETFs provide transparency and flexibility in their portfolio construction. Unlike actively managed funds, smart beta ETFs disclose their holdings on a regular basis, allowing investors to see exactly what they are investing in. Additionally, smart beta ETFs typically have lower fees compared to actively managed funds, making them a cost-effective way to gain exposure to specific factors or investment themes.

There are several different types of smart beta ETFs available to investors, each with its own unique strategy and focus. Some smart beta ETFs may focus on value stocks that are trading at a discount to their intrinsic value, while others may target high-quality companies with strong fundamentals and sustainable earnings growth. Still, others may focus on momentum stocks that have exhibited strong price performance in recent months.

Investors interested in smart beta ETFs should carefully consider their investment objectives, risk tolerance, and time horizon before investing. While smart beta ETFs can offer the potential for outperformance compared to traditional ETFs, they also carry additional risks, such as factor concentration and tracking error. As with any investment, it is important to conduct thorough research and due diligence before adding smart beta ETFs to your portfolio.

In conclusion, smart beta ETFs offer investors a unique and innovative approach to investing in the stock market. By combining the benefits of both passive and active investing strategies, smart beta ETFs seek to provide superior risk-adjusted returns over the long term. With a wide range of strategies and themes to choose from, investors can tailor their portfolios to meet their individual investment goals and objectives. As always, it is important to consult with a financial advisor before making any investment decisions to ensure that smart beta ETFs are suitable for your specific needs and circumstances.

10.Leveraged and Inverse ETFs

One type of ETF that has gained significant traction in recent years is leveraged and inverse ETFs. These ETFs are designed to provide investors with the ability to amplify their returns or profit from a decline in the underlying asset or index. Leveraged ETFs use derivatives and debt to magnify the returns of a specific index or asset, whereas inverse ETFs seek to profit from the decline in the value of an underlying asset or index.

Leveraged ETFs

Leveraged ETFs are designed to track the daily performance of an underlying asset or index with a multiple greater than one. For example, a 2x leveraged ETF seeks to double the daily return of the underlying asset or index. Leveraged ETFs are popular among investors who want to magnify their returns through the use of leverage.

While leveraged ETFs can provide investors with the opportunity to amplify their returns, they also come with increased risks. Due to the compounding effect of leverage, leveraged ETFs can experience amplified losses if the underlying asset or index experiences a significant decline. Additionally, leveraged ETFs are designed to track the daily performance of the underlying asset or index, which can lead to tracking errors over longer periods of time.

Investors interested in leveraged ETFs should carefully consider their investment objectives, risk tolerance, and investment time horizon before investing in these products. It is important for investors to understand the risks associated with leverage and to use leveraged ETFs as a part of a diversified investment portfolio.

Inverse ETFs

Inverse ETFs are designed to profit from the decline in the value of an underlying asset or index. These ETFs use derivatives such as futures contracts and options to achieve an inverse relationship with the underlying asset or index. For example, a -1x inverse ETF seeks to provide the opposite performance of the underlying asset or index, meaning that if the underlying asset or index declines by 1%, the ETF will increase by 1%.

Inverse ETFs are popular among investors who want to hedge their portfolio against a decline in the value of specific assets or indices. These ETFs can be used by investors to profit from market downturns or to protect their portfolio against potential losses.

Like leveraged ETFs, inverse ETFs come with increased risks. Due to the use of derivatives and leverage, inverse ETFs can experience amplified losses if the underlying asset or index experiences a significant increase in value. Additionally, inverse ETFs are designed to provide the opposite performance of the underlying asset or index on a daily basis, which can lead to tracking errors over longer periods of time.

Investors interested in inverse ETFs should carefully consider their investment objectives, risk tolerance, and investment time horizon before investing in these products. It is important for investors to understand the risks associated with inverse ETFs and to use these products as a part of a diversified investment strategy.

Leveraged and inverse ETFs can provide investors with the opportunity to amplify their returns or profit from a decline in the value of specific assets or indices. These ETFs offer investors the ability to access complex investment strategies such as leverage and inverse exposure in a convenient and cost-effective manner.

However, it is important for investors to

carefully evaluate the risks associated with leveraged and inverse ETFs before investing in these products. Leveraged and inverse ETFs come with increased risks due to the use of leverage and derivatives, which can lead to amplified losses in certain market conditions.

Investors should consider their investment objectives, risk tolerance, and investment time horizon before investing in leveraged and inverse ETFs. It is recommended to consult with a financial advisor or investment professional before investing in these products to ensure that they are suitable for your investment goals and risk profile.

In conclusion, leveraged and inverse ETFs can be powerful investment tools for investors seeking to amplify their returns or profit from a decline in the value of specific assets or indices. However, these ETFs come with increased risks that investors should be aware of before investing in them. It is important for investors to conduct thorough research and due diligence before investing in leveraged and inverse ETFs to ensure that they align with their investment objectives and risk tolerance.

11. How to choose ETFs evaluate ETF liquidity

With the growing popularity of ETFs, there are now thousands of options available to investors, making the choice of which ETF to invest in a daunting task. One important factor to consider when selecting an ETF is its liquidity. In this article, we will discuss the importance of ETF liquidity and how to evaluate the liquidity of ETFs.

What is ETF Liquidity?

Liquidity refers to the ease with which an asset can be bought or sold in the market without significantly impacting its price. An ETF is considered liquid if there is a high volume of trading activity in the ETF, which allows investors to buy or sell shares of the ETF quickly and at a fair price. On the other hand, an ETF is illiquid if there is low trading volume, making it difficult for investors to buy or sell shares without experiencing price fluctuations or facing challenges in executing trades.

Why is ETF Liquidity Important?

ETF liquidity is important for several reasons. First and foremost, liquidity ensures that investors can easily enter and exit their positions in an ETF without incurring significant costs or price distortions. Liquid ETFs typically have tight bid-ask spreads, which is the difference between the price at which an investor can sell an ETF (the bid price) and the price at which an investor can buy an ETF (the ask price). Narrow bid-ask spreads indicate that the ETF is liquid and that investors can buy or sell shares at a fair price.

Additionally, liquidity is important for risk management. In times of market stress or volatility, illiquid ETFs may experience wider bid-ask spreads, making it more challenging for investors to trade them without incurring losses. Moreover, illiquid ETFs may have limited trading volume, which can result in difficulty in executing trades and potentially lead to significant price discrepancies between the ETF's net asset value (NAV) and its market price.

How to Evaluate ETF Liquidity?

There are several factors to consider when evaluating the liquidity of an ETF:

Trading Volume: One of the key metrics to assess ETF liquidity is its average daily trading volume. The trading volume represents the number of shares of the ETF that are bought and sold on a daily basis. Higher trading volume typically indicates greater liquidity, as there are more market participants actively trading the ETF.

Bid-Ask Spread: The bid-ask spread is another

important indicator of ETF liquidity. A narrow bid-ask spread indicates that the ETF is liquid, as there is minimal difference between the price at which investors can buy and sell the ETF. Wide bid-ask spreads may suggest that the ETF is illiquid, leading to potential price discrepancies and higher trading costs.

Market Makers: Market makers play a crucial role in ensuring liquidity in the ETF market. These firms provide liquidity by continuously quoting bid and ask prices for ETFs and facilitating the buying and selling of shares. The presence of market makers can help improve the liquidity of an ETF and tighten bid-ask spreads.

Primary Market: The primary market for ETFs is where new shares of the ETF are created and redeemed. The ability of authorized participants (APs) to create and redeem shares in the primary market helps maintain the liquidity of the ETF. If there is consistent demand for the ETF, APs can create new shares to meet investor demand, thus ensuring liquidity in the secondary market.

Tracking Error: Tracking error measures how closely an ETF's performance tracks its underlying index. High tracking error may be a sign of lower liquidity, as the ETF may struggle to accurately replicate the index due to trading inefficiencies or liquidity issues.

Evaluating the liquidity of an ETF is a critical step in the investment decision-making process. Liquid ETFs provide investors with the flexibility to enter and exit positions quickly and at a fair price, while minimizing trading costs and price discrepancies. By considering factors such as trading volume, bid-ask spread, market makers, primary market activity, and tracking error, investors can assess the liquidity of an ETF and make informed investment decisions. Remember, a liquid ETF is key to a successful and efficient investment strategy.

12. Analyzing the costs of ETFs

An ETF, or Exchange-Traded Fund, is a popular investment tool that provides investors with the opportunity to diversify their portfolios through a single security. Unlike mutual funds, ETFs are traded on stock exchanges just like individual stocks, making them a convenient and cost-effective option for investors looking to gain exposure to a diverse range of assets.

One of the key advantages of ETFs is their low cost structure. But while ETFs are generally known for their low expense ratios, it's important for investors to understand the full range of costs associated with these funds in order to make informed investment decisions.

In this article, we will explore the various costs associated with ETFs and provide investors with a comprehensive guide to analyzing these costs.

Expense Ratios: The most widely cited cost associated with ETFs is the expense ratio, which represents the annual operating expenses of the fund as a percentage of its total assets. Expense ratios typically range from 0.05% to 1.00% or higher, with the average expense ratio for ETFs hovering around 0.44%.

It's important for investors to pay attention to expense ratios because they can have a significant impact on investment returns over time. Lower expense ratios generally translate to higher returns for investors, as a lower percentage of the fund's assets are being spent on operating expenses.

Tracking Error: Another cost that investors should be aware of when analyzing ETFs is tracking error. Tracking error represents the discrepancy between the performance of the

ETF and the performance of its underlying index. While tracking error is not a direct fee that investors pay, it can impact the overall returns of the fund.

Investors should look for ETFs with low tracking error, as this indicates that the fund is closely tracking its benchmark index. High tracking error can erode returns over time, so it's important for investors to consider this cost when evaluating ETFs.

Bid-Ask Spread: When trading ETFs, investors are exposed to the bid-ask spread, which represents the difference between the price at which an investor can buy and sell shares of the fund. The bid-ask spread is essentially a trading cost that can impact the overall returns of an ETF investment.

For highly liquid ETFs with tight bid-ask spreads, trading costs are minimal. However, for less liquid ETFs with wider spreads, investors may incur higher trading costs. It's important for investors to be mindful of the bid-ask spread when buying and selling ETFs in order to minimize trading costs.

Brokerage Commissions: Investors should also consider brokerage commissions when analyzing the costs of ETFs. While many brokerage firms offer commission-free trading for select ETFs, investors may still incur trading costs when buying and selling shares of ETFs not included in these programs.

Investors should be aware of the brokerage commission structure of their chosen brokerage firm and factor these costs into their overall investment strategy. Choosing a brokerage firm that offers commission-free trading for a wide range of ETFs can help investors minimize costs and optimize their investment returns.

Taxes: Finally, investors should consider the

tax implications of investing in ETFs. ETFs are known for their tax efficiency, as they generally have lower capital gains distributions compared to mutual funds. However, it's important for investors to be aware of any potential tax liabilities associated with their ETF investments.

Investors should consult with a tax advisor to fully understand the tax implications of investing in ETFs and develop a tax-efficient investment strategy. By considering taxes as a cost of investing in ETFs, investors can optimize their after-tax returns and achieve their long-term financial goals.

Analyzing the costs of ETFs is essential for investors looking to build a diversified and cost-effective investment portfolio. By considering expense ratios, tracking error, bid-ask spreads, brokerage commissions, and taxes, investors can make informed decisions and maximize their investment returns.

It's important for investors to conduct thorough research and due diligence when evaluating ETFs in order to understand the full range of costs associated with these funds. By taking a comprehensive approach to analyzing the costs of ETFs, investors can build a well-balanced investment portfolio that aligns with their financial objectives and risk tolerance.

13.Consider diversifying your ETFs

Considering ETF Diversification

Exchange-traded funds (ETFs) have become increasingly popular investment vehicles for both individual investors and institutions due to their simplicity, transparency, and low cost. ETFs offer investors exposure to a diversified portfolio of assets, which can help reduce risk and enhance returns. However, it is important for investors to consider the diversification of their ETF holdings in order to optimize their investment portfolio.

Diversification is a fundamental principle of investing that involves spreading your investments across different asset classes, industries, and geographical regions to reduce risk and enhance returns. By diversifying your portfolio, you can mitigate the impact of a decline in any one asset class or sector and potentially improve your overall investment performance.

When it comes to investing in ETFs, diversification is equally important. While ETFs already provide investors with exposure to a diversified portfolio of assets, it is important to consider how your ETF holdings are diversified across different asset classes, sectors, and geographical regions.

One way to achieve diversification with ETFs is to invest in a broad-based ETF that tracks a major stock market index, such as the S&P 500 or the MSCI World Index. These types of ETFs provide investors with exposure to a wide range of stocks across different industries and sectors, which can help reduce concentration risk.

Another way to diversify your ETF holdings is to invest in ETFs that focus on specific asset classes or sectors, such as technology, healthcare, or real estate. By adding these sector-specific ETFs to your portfolio, you can further diversify your investments and potentially enhance your returns.

It is also important to consider geographical diversification when investing in ETFs. Investing in ETFs that track international stock markets can help reduce the correlation between your investments and the domestic market, providing you with additional diversification benefits.

Furthermore, investors should consider the correlation between their ETF holdings when constructing their investment portfolio. Correlation measures the degree to which two assets move in relation to each other. By investing in ETFs with low correlation to each other, investors can achieve better diversification benefits and reduce portfolio risk.

When selecting ETFs for your investment

portfolio, it is important to consider your investment objectives, risk tolerance, and time horizon. For example, investors with a long-term investment horizon may consider investing in a mix of equity and fixed-income ETFs to achieve a balance between risk and return. On the other hand, investors with a shorter time horizon may focus on more conservative ETFs, such as bond ETFs, to preserve capital.

In addition to considering diversification within your ETF holdings, it is also important to regularly review and rebalance your portfolio to maintain optimal diversification. Over time, the performance of different asset classes and sectors may vary, leading to changes in the overall composition of your portfolio. By rebalancing your portfolio periodically, you can ensure that your investments remain aligned with your investment objectives and risk tolerance.

Overall, diversification is a key component of

successful investing, and ETFs offer investors a convenient and cost-effective way to achieve diversification in their investment portfolios. By considering how your ETF holdings are diversified across different asset classes, sectors, and geographical regions, you can optimize your investment portfolio, reduce risk, and potentially enhance returns. Remember to regularly review and rebalance your portfolio to maintain optimal diversification and achieve your investment goals.

14. Evaluate the historical performance of ETFs

One of the key reasons for the popularity of ETFs is their low cost relative to actively managed mutual funds. ETFs typically have lower expense ratios than mutual funds, making them an attractive option for cost-conscious investors. In addition, ETFs are traded on stock exchanges, which means that they can be bought and sold throughout the trading day, providing investors with greater liquidity and flexibility compared to traditional mutual funds.

But while ETFs offer many advantages, investors need to carefully evaluate the historical performance of these investment vehicles before deciding to include them in their portfolios. By analyzing the historical performance of ETFs, investors can gain valuable insights into how these funds have performed in different market conditions and make informed decisions about whether or not to invest in them.

One of the key factors that investors should consider when evaluating the historical performance of ETFs is the fund's tracking error. Tracking error measures the extent to which an ETF's returns deviate from those of its underlying index. A low tracking error indicates that the ETF closely tracks its benchmark index, while a high tracking error suggests that the ETF may not be providing the expected returns.

Another important metric to consider when evaluating the historical performance of ETFs is the fund's historical returns. By analyzing the historical returns of an ETF, investors can get a sense of how the fund has performed over time and whether it has been able to generate positive returns for investors. It is important to consider not only the overall returns of the ETF, but also how these returns have compared to the returns of its benchmark index and other similar funds.

In addition to tracking error and historical returns, investors should also consider other factors that may impact the performance of ETFs. These factors include the fund's expense ratio, trading volume, and liquidity, as well as the composition of the underlying index and the fund's sector and geographic exposure.

Furthermore, investors should take into account the fund's performance relative to its peer group and benchmark index. By comparing the performance of an ETF to that of similar funds and benchmark indices, investors can assess whether the fund has outperformed or underperformed its peers and determine whether it is likely to continue to do so in the future.

It is also important for investors to consider the risk profile of ETFs when evaluating their historical performance. Different ETFs may have different levels of risk depending on the assets they hold and the investment strategies they employ. By assessing the historical risk-adjusted returns of ETFs, investors can gain a better understanding of the risk-return profile of these funds and determine whether they are suitable for their investment objectives and risk tolerance.

Evaluating the historical performance of ETFs is an essential step for investors looking to include these funds in their portfolios. By analyzing metrics such as tracking error, historical returns, expense ratios, trading volume, and risk-adjusted returns, investors can make informed decisions about which ETFs to invest in and how to allocate their assets effectively. ETFs offer numerous benefits for investors, but it is crucial to conduct thorough research and analysis before making investment decisions to ensure that these funds will meet their long-term investment goals.

15.Examine the underlying of the ETF

ETFs, or Exchange Traded Funds, offer a wide range of investment opportunities, allowing investors to easily diversify their portfolio at a low cost. However, before investing in an ETF, it is important to examine the underlying of the ETF to better understand how it works and what potential risks and opportunities are involved.

The underlying of an ETF is the index, commodity, sector, or asset that the ETF seeks to replicate or track. For example, an ETF based on the S&P 500 will have the S&P 500 index as its underlying, while an ETF based on gold will have the price of gold as its underlying. Examining the underlying of the ETF is important because it will determine the performance and volatility of the ETF itself. Additionally, understanding the underlying of the ETF can help investors assess whether the ETF is suitable for their investment objectives and risk profile.

One of the main advantages of investing in ETFs is diversification. ETFs allow investors to diversify across various assets or sectors without having to purchase individual stocks or securities. However, it is important to note that even though an ETF is diversified, there are still risks associated with the underlying of the ETF.

For example, if the ETF is based on a single sector or stock, the investor is exposed to the specific risk of that sector or stock. If the underlying of the ETF experiences a significant price fluctuation due to external or internal factors, the ETF will also undergo a price fluctuation. Therefore, it is important for investors to carefully examine the underlying of the ETF to evaluate the potential risks and opportunities.

Another important aspect to consider when examining the underlying of an ETF is the method of index replication. ETFs can replicate or track the performance of the underlying in different ways, such as through a physical or synthetic approach. An ETF with physical replication actually holds the underlying assets, while an ETF with synthetic replication uses financial derivatives to gain exposure to the underlying.

Each approach has its own risks and benefits. ETFs with physical replication tend to be more transparent and closely track the performance of the underlying, but may incur higher costs. ETFs with synthetic replication, on the other hand, may be more cost-effective, but there are risks associated with the counterparty providing the financial derivative.

Lastly, it is also important to examine the ETF manager and their track record. ETF managers are responsible for efficiently managing the ETF portfolio and replicating the underlying as faithfully as possible. Investors should consider the ETF's past performance, as well as the expertise and experience of the ETF manager.

Examining the underlying of an ETF is essential for investors who want to better understand how the ETF works and what potential risks and opportunities are involved. Before investing in an ETF, investors should carefully evaluate the underlying, the method of index replication, the ETF manager, and their track record. With a thorough evaluation of the underlying of the ETF, investors can make informed decisions and improve their chances of success in the financial market.

16. Capital gains and losses of the ETF

In recent years, Exchange-Traded Funds (ETFs) have become increasingly popular among investors looking for a low-cost and efficient way to gain exposure to a wide range of assets. ETFs are investment funds that are listed on stock exchanges and trade like individual stocks. They provide investors with a way to diversify their portfolios without having to buy individual securities.

There are several advantages to investing in ETFs. One of the main benefits is their low cost. ETFs typically have lower expense ratios compared to traditional mutual funds, making them an attractive option for cost-conscious investors. Additionally, ETFs are highly liquid, meaning they can be bought and sold throughout the trading day at market price. This provides investors with flexibility and allows them to react quickly to changing market conditions.

Another advantage of ETFs is their tax efficiency. Because ETFs are structured as open-end investment companies, they are able to minimize capital gains distributions to shareholders. This can lead to lower tax liabilities for investors, making ETFs a tax-efficient investment vehicle.

ETFs also provide investors with a high level of transparency. Unlike traditional mutual funds, which are only required to disclose their holdings on a quarterly basis, ETFs are required to disclose their holdings on a daily basis. This level of transparency allows investors to know exactly what they are investing in and helps them make more informed decisions about their portfolios.

Despite the many advantages of investing in ETFs, there are also some drawbacks to consider. One potential downside is the lack of flexibility in actively managing investments. ETFs are passively managed, meaning they track an underlying index or benchmark and do not actively buy or sell securities in an attempt to outperform the market. While this can result in lower costs, it also means that investors have limited control over the investments held within the ETF.

Another potential disadvantage of ETFs is their exposure to market risk. Because ETFs track a specific index or sector, they are subject to the same market fluctuations as the underlying assets. This can lead to volatility in the value of the ETF, which may be a concern for more risk-averse investors.

Additionally, the structure of ETFs can have some unique risks. For example, because ETFs are traded on stock exchanges, they are subject to market forces that can impact their price. This can lead to price discrepancies between the value of the ETF and the value of its underlying assets, known as the ETF's net asset value (NAV).

ETFs offer investors a number of advantages, including low cost, high liquidity, tax efficiency, and transparency. However, investors should also be aware of the potential drawbacks, such as limited control over investments, exposure to market risk, and the unique risks associated with the structure of ETFs. By carefully weighing the pros and cons of investing in ETFs, investors can make informed decisions about whether these investment vehicles are right for their portfolios.

17.The harmonized ETFs and the non-harmonized ETFs

In this article we will examine the differences between the two and discuss their distinctive characteristics.

Harmonized ETFs are exchange-traded funds that follow specific rules established by regulatory bodies, such as the European Union. These rules set minimum standards that ETFs must adhere to in order to be considered harmonized. These standards mainly concern transparency, liquidity, and diversification of the ETF. Harmonized ETFs are regulated to ensure that investors have access to complete and up-to-date information on the underlying assets of the ETF and that the ETF is sufficiently liquid to allow investors to easily enter and exit their position.

Non-harmonized ETFs, on the other hand, are not subject to the same rules and regulatory standards as harmonized funds. These ETFs may be structured in different ways and may not offer the same level of transparency, liquidity, or diversification as harmonized ETFs. Non-harmonized ETFs may be riskier for investors, as they may not be subject to the same level of oversight and regulation by supervisory authorities.

One of the main differences between harmonized and non-harmonized ETFs is that harmonized ETFs are regulated under a set of rules and directives established in Europe, which ensure a certain standard of protection for investors. Non-harmonized ETFs, on the other hand, may be based on local regulations or may be structured in a very different way, depending on the ETF provider and the market on which it is listed.

Another significant difference between the two types of ETF is their transparency. Harmonized ETFs are required to provide complete and transparent information about their underlying assets, allowing investors to have a clear view of the stocks, bonds, or commodities in which the ETF is invested. Non-harmonized ETFs may not offer the same level of transparency, making it more difficult for investors to assess the risk and potential return of the ETF.

Liquidity is another important issue to consider when evaluating the difference between harmonized and non-harmonized ETFs. Harmonized ETFs are designed to be liquid enough to allow investors to easily buy and sell ETF shares on the open market. Non-harmonized ETFs may not offer the same level of liquidity, which could make it more difficult for investors to enter and exit their position without suffering significant losses.

Finally, diversification is another key difference between harmonized and non-harmonized ETFs. Harmonized ETFs are designed to be well diversified, in order to reduce risk for investors. Non-harmonized ETFs may not offer the same level of diversification, which could expose investors to greater risks if a particular sector or asset were to experience a sharp market correction.

Harmonized and non-harmonized ETFs present significant differences in how they are structured, regulated, and managed. Harmonized ETFs offer investors greater transparency, liquidity, and diversification, making them a safer and more reliable choice for those looking to invest in exchange-traded funds. Non-harmonized ETFs, on the other hand, may offer more flexible and diversified investment opportunities, but they may also expose investors to greater risks. Before investing in an ETF, it is important to carefully evaluate the product's characteristics and its level of regulation to ensure that it meets your needs and investment objectives.

18.Opening a trading account through your online bank if it offers the service and evaluating commission costs

In recent years, online trading has gained more and more space among Italian investors, thanks to the convenience and practicality of being able to operate directly from one's own home or from anywhere in the world, thanks to technology and increasingly advanced and intuitive online trading platforms.

One of the most common operations in online trading is opening a trading account with an online bank or a specialized online broker. This operation allows you to invest in various financial instruments, including ETFs (Exchange Traded Funds), which are investment funds that replicate the performance of a reference index and offer various low-cost and diversified investment opportunities.

But how do you open an online trading account and what are the costs to consider when investing in ETFs? In this article, we will examine in detail the steps to follow to open an online trading account and evaluate commission costs for investing in ETFs.

Steps to open an online trading account

The first step in opening an online trading account is to choose the platform or online bank where you want to open the account. It is important to do thorough research to find a reliable and regulated intermediary that offers a wide range of ETFs and financial instruments, competitive fees, and a user-friendly interface.

Once you have chosen the platform, you will need to fill out an online registration form with your personal, tax, and financial data. In some cases, you may be asked to provide identification and proof of residence. Once registration is complete, you will need to make an initial deposit into the trading account in order to start investing.

After completing these steps, you can start navigating the trading platform and investing in the selection of available ETFs. It is important to familiarize yourself with the interface and features of the platform in order to operate effectively and responsibly.

Costs to consider when investing in ETFs

Before investing in ETFs, it is important to evaluate the commission costs charged by the trading platform or your online bank. Commissions may vary based on the type of ETF, trading frequency, and investment volume.

The main commissions to consider when investing in ETFs are:

- Trading commission: this is the commission charged by the platform or broker for each ETF purchase or sale transaction. This commission may be fixed or variable based on investment volume.

- Management fee: this is the annual fee that the ETF charges to cover fund management costs. This fee is deducted directly from the ETF's value and may vary based on the type of fund and management company.

- Custodial fee: this is the fee charged by the platform or broker for custody of ETFs in the trading account. This fee may be monthly, annual, or based on investment volume.

It is important to carefully evaluate these commissions to choose the most cost-effective and suitable trading platform for your investment needs.

Opening an online trading account to invest in

ETFs is a simple and convenient operation that allows you to diversify your portfolio and access a wide range of investment opportunities. It is important to carefully evaluate commission costs to trade responsibly and cost-effectively. With a bit of research and practice, you can achieve excellent results in online trading and investing in ETFs.

19.Choosing the ETF trading platform

Choosing the right ETF trading platform is a crucial step for investors who want to enter the world of Exchange-Traded Funds. With the increasing popularity of ETFs as an investment tool, it is essential to find the right platform that meets your needs and financial goals.

ETFs also offer high liquidity, as they can be bought and sold at any time during the trading session, just like stocks. This flexibility makes them particularly suitable for investors who want greater agility in managing their portfolio.

To choose the ETF trading platform that best suits your needs, it is important to take into consideration a number of key factors. Firstly, it is essential to evaluate the platform's ease of use and its intuitiveness. Investors, both experienced and beginners, should be able to navigate easily through the various features and tools offered by the platform.

Another important feature to consider is the availability of research and analysis tools. A good ETF trading platform should offer a wide range of technical and fundamental analysis tools to support investors in making their investment decisions. Additionally, the platform should provide real-time market news and updates on the performance of ETFs and benchmark indices.

The quality of customer service is another crucial aspect to consider when choosing an ETF trading platform. Investors should be able to quickly and easily contact customer service for assistance in case of problems or questions. It is important to ensure that the platform offers timely and professional customer support to ensure a good trading experience.

Furthermore, it is essential to consider the fees and costs associated with the ETF trading platform. Investors should carefully evaluate trading fees, management fees, and any other expenses to ensure they are getting a good value for their money. It is advisable to compare different platforms to find the one that offers the most advantageous conditions based on your investment style and budget.

Lastly, it is important to assess the security and reliability of the ETF trading platform. Investors should ensure that the platform adopts robust security measures to protect user funds and personal data. It is advisable to choose a regulated platform with a good reputation in the industry to minimize the risks of fraud or scams.

In conclusion, choosing the right ETF trading platform is a crucial step for investors who want to capitalize on the potential of Exchange-Traded Funds. Carefully evaluating the various aspects discussed in this article will help investors find the platform that best suits their needs and financial goals, allowing them to make the most of the opportunities offered by ETFs.

In an increasingly digitalized world, with a wide range of trading platforms available, it is important to make a thoughtful choice to achieve the best possible results in your investment journey. Selecting the most suitable platform can truly make a difference in reaching your financial goals.

20.Investment Planning in ETFs

For investments in ETFs, it is essential to have a detailed and well-researched plan.

Investment planning in ETFs is a process that requires time, research, and discipline. Before investing in ETFs, it is important to have a clear understanding of your financial goals, your time horizon, and your risk tolerance. Additionally, you should consider various factors such as ETF costs, past performance, and benchmark index volatility.

One of the first things to do when planning investments in ETFs is to identify your long-term financial goals. Whether it is saving for retirement, children's education, or buying a house, it is important to have clear financial goals before starting to invest. Once you have identified your goals, you can establish an investment plan that takes into account these goals and your time horizon.

After identifying your financial goals, it is important to assess your risk tolerance. ETFs are often considered low-risk investments, as they replicate the performance of a benchmark index. However, it is important to remember that investing in ETFs still carries a risk of capital loss. Before investing in ETFs, it is essential to evaluate your risk tolerance and ensure that you are comfortable with the potential risk and volatility of the benchmark index.

Once you have identified your financial goals and assessed your risk tolerance, it is important to conduct thorough research on the ETFs available in the market. There are thousands of ETFs available, investing in a wide range of sectors and asset classes. Before investing in an ETF, it is important to consider various factors such as ETF costs, past performance, and benchmark index volatility. Additionally, it is important to also evaluate the liquidity and size of the ETF to ensure that it is suitable for your investment needs.

Once you have identified ETFs that fit your financial goals, risk tolerance, and research, it is important to establish an investment plan. This plan should take into account your time horizon, financial goals, and risk tolerance. Additionally, it is important to consider diversifying your portfolio by investing in different sectors and asset classes to reduce the risk of capital loss.

When planning investments in ETFs, it is also important to consider the costs associated with the investment. ETFs have management expenses, known as expense ratios, which can range from 0.05% to 1% of the investment value. It is important to consider these costs when choosing an ETF, as they can affect investment returns in the long term.

Finally, it is important to constantly monitor your investments in ETFs and make any changes to your investment plan based on market conditions and changes in your financial goals. Investment planning in ETFs is a continuous process that requires discipline and attention to detail.

Investment planning in ETFs is a process that requires time, research, and discipline. Before investing in ETFs, it is important to identify your financial goals, assess your risk tolerance, conduct thorough research on available ETFs, establish an investment plan, and constantly monitor your investments. With the right planning, investments in ETFs can be an excellent option to diversify your portfolio and maximize your long-term returns.

Monitoring Investments in ETFs

Exchange-Traded Funds (ETFs) are financial instruments that track the performance of a market index, a commodity, or a specific sector. ETFs offer several advantages over traditional investments in stocks or bonds, including greater liquidity, intrinsic diversification, and lower costs. However, to maximize returns on investments in ETFs, it is essential to constantly monitor the portfolio and make adjustments based on market conditions.

Monitoring investments in ETFs is an ongoing process that requires good planning and a solid investment strategy. Before investing in ETFs, it is important to identify the financial goals and risk profile of the investor. Based on this information, it is possible to select the most suitable ETFs for one's needs and build a diversified portfolio.

Once the ETF portfolio is created, it is essential to constantly monitor the performance of individual funds and the entire portfolio. To do this, various tools and indicators can be used, such as market charts, financial reports, and expert analysis. Additionally, it is important to consider macroeconomic and political events that could influence financial markets and therefore investments in ETFs.

Another crucial aspect of monitoring investments in ETFs is evaluating the portfolio's performance. To assess the returns of ETFs, it is possible to compare investments with a benchmark market index or with other similar portfolios. Furthermore, it is important to analyze the costs and fees incurred for ETF investments in order to maximize net returns.

In the process of monitoring investments in ETFs, it is also important to consider risk management. To protect invested capital, various risk management strategies can be used, such as using stop-loss orders, diversifying the portfolio, and allocating assets based on the investor's risk tolerance.

Finally, it is essential to be flexible in monitoring investments in ETFs and make adjustments based on market conditions. If the performance of ETFs does not meet expectations or significant changes occur in market conditions, it may be necessary to reallocate the portfolio or modify the investment strategy.

Monitoring investments in ETFs is a fundamental process to maximize returns and protect invested capital. With good planning, a solid investment strategy, and constant vigilance, positive results can be achieved and financial goals can be reached.

21. A distribution ETF that releases dividends

One of the most interesting features of dividend distributing ETFs is the ability to release dividends to investors. These dividends can be a source of regular income for investors, allowing them to benefit from the profits generated by the companies contained in the ETF.

The companies included in a dividend distributing ETF are selected based on criteria established by the fund manager and may vary depending on the investment objective of the ETF. For example, a dividend distributing ETF that tracks the performance of the S&P 500 index will contain shares of the companies included in that index, while a dividend distributing ETF that aims to follow the technology sector will include shares of technology companies.

Once a dividend distributing ETF generates profits from the companies included in the fund, the fund manager may decide to distribute these profits to investors in the form of dividends. These dividends can be paid monthly, quarterly, or annually, depending on the distribution policy of the ETF.

It is important to note that dividend distributing ETFs are not guaranteed to release dividends and returns may vary depending on the performance of the companies included in the fund. However, many investors find dividend distributing ETFs attractive for the possibility of obtaining a regular income without having to select and monitor individual stocks or bonds.

For example, an investor who wishes to build a diversified portfolio of blue-chip stocks and high-yield bonds could opt for a dividend distributing ETF that includes a wide range of securities in both categories. This approach allows the investor to benefit from the dividends generated by these companies without having to purchase and manage each stock individually.

Another advantage of dividend distributing ETFs is the transparency and liquidity offered by these instruments. ETFs are traded on the stock exchange like stocks and can be easily bought and sold during market hours. This allows investors to adjust their portfolio quickly and efficiently based on market conditions and investment objectives.

Additionally, dividend distributing ETFs offer greater diversification compared to direct investments in individual stocks or bonds. Since an ETF contains a wide range of securities, investors are exposed to lower risk compared to investing in a single company. This can help reduce overall portfolio volatility and protect investors from market fluctuations.

It should be noted that dividend distributing ETFs may incur some expenses, such as management fees and trading fees. Before investing in a dividend distributing ETF, it is important to carefully evaluate the fees associated with the fund and compare them with potential returns to ensure that the investment is suitable for one's financial needs.

Dividend distributing ETFs can be an interesting option for investors looking to generate regular income from a diversified portfolio of stocks and bonds. These instruments offer transparency, liquidity, and diversification, allowing investors to benefit from the dividends generated by the companies included in the ETF. Before investing in a dividend distributing ETF, it is important to carefully evaluate the costs and compare them with potential returns to ensure that the investment is suitable for one's financial needs.

22.ETF accumulation

Accumulation ETFs and how do they work? In this article we will take a closer look at these particular types of ETFs, analyzing the pros and cons and providing some tips on how to use them in your investment portfolio.

Accumulation ETFs are a type of exchange-traded fund that automatically reinvests dividends or interest earned, rather than distributing them to investors. In practice, the profits generated from the buying and selling of the underlying assets are reinvested in the fund itself, increasing its net asset value (NAV) and the price of the shares.

This mechanism allows investors to benefit from compound interest, as the accumulated gains are reinvested in the fund at no additional cost. Furthermore, accumulation ETFs offer greater tax efficiency compared to traditional distribution funds, as no taxes are generated on dividends until the investor sells their shares.

I strongly recommend the choice of accumulation ETFs over distribution ones

Another important advantage of accumulation ETFs is greater transparency and liquidity compared to traditional mutual funds. Being traded on the stock exchange, ETFs can be bought and sold at any time, perhaps liquidating only a portion of the share or the total depending on the needs during the trading day, allowing investors to manage their portfolio more flexibly.

That being said, accumulation ETFs are not without disadvantages. One of the main risks is related to market volatility, which can significantly affect the price of the ETF shares. If the market undergoes a significant correction, the value of the accumulation ETF could undergo a sharp decline, causing losses to investors.

To make the most of accumulation ETFs, it is important to consider several aspects. First of all, it is advisable to create a diversified portfolio that includes a variety of asset classes and market sectors, in order to reduce concentration risk and increase portfolio resilience.

Secondly, it is important to carefully monitor the market performance and the chosen accumulation ETF, in order to assess any buying or selling opportunities based on market conditions and investment needs.

Finally, it is important to pay attention to the costs associated with accumulation ETFs and try to minimize management and trading fees, in order to maximize long-term returns.

Accumulation ETFs represent an interesting investment opportunity for investors who want to benefit from compound interest and diversification offered by these financial instruments. Before investing in an accumulation ETF, it is important to carefully evaluate the pros and cons and try to maximize long-term returns.

The Advantage of Compound Interest in Accumulation ETFs

Accumulation ETFs offer their holders the opportunity to achieve higher returns in the long term compared to distribution ETFs. In this chapter, we will examine the advantages of compound interest and how investors can benefit from it.

Before getting into the details, it is important to understand what compound interest is. In simple terms, it is a process that allows reinvested returns to generate new returns over time. This means that gains are not distributed to ETF holders, but automatically reinvested to increase the initial capital.

Compound interest ETFs are particularly advantageous for long-term investors because they allow them to benefit from the snowball effect. In other words, the longer the returns are reinvested, the greater the multiplier effect.

One of the most interesting aspects of compound interest is its ability to generate exponential gains over time. For example, if an investor holds a compound interest ETF for 10 years and the annual returns are around 5%, their initial capital could grow significantly thanks to the snowball effect.

Furthermore, compound interest ETFs offer greater diversification to investors. Since returns are automatically reinvested, the ETF can acquire a greater variety of assets and therefore reduce the overall risk of the portfolio.

Another important feature of compound interest ETFs is their ease of management. Since returns are automatically reinvested, investors do not have to worry about deciding how to reinvest their gains. This allows them to focus on more important decisions, such as choosing which assets to invest in or the duration of the investment.

Finally, compound interest ETFs offer greater transparency to investors. Since returns are automatically reinvested, it is easier to monitor the performance of their investment over time and understand how gains are accumulating.

In summary, compound interest ETFs are an excellent choice for investors looking to maximize their returns in the long term. Thanks to the ability to benefit from the snowball effect, greater diversification, ease of management, and transparency, investors can achieve superior results compared to distribution ETFs.

If you are interested in investing in compound interest ETFs, with the right strategy and planning, compound interest ETFs can be a great tool to grow your wealth over time.

23.Investment Strategies

Stock ETFs are an increasingly popular investment tool among investors, thanks to their diversified and transparent nature. For those looking to achieve attractive returns while reducing investment risk, stock ETFs represent a very interesting option.

But what are the possibilities of earning by investing in stock ETFs and how is it possible to achieve a return of over 20% per year? In this article, we will explore the potential and risks of investing in stock ETFs and provide helpful tips to maximize returns.

Why invest in stock ETFs?

Stock ETFs represent an effective way to invest in stocks of different companies, reducing concentration risk and improving portfolio diversification. With a basket of stocks within a single instrument, ETFs offer investors the opportunity to participate in the potential appreciation of the stock market as a whole without having to choose and monitor individual stocks.

Furthermore, stock ETFs offer lower management costs compared to mutual funds and investment trusts, making them a cost-effective choice for investors looking to maximize net returns.

How to achieve a return of over 20% per year?

Many ETFs, for example, that invest in the S&P 500 (top companies in the United States) and global stocks in the MSCI World, can have returns exceeding 20%.

Achieving a return of over 20% per year by investing in stock ETFs is possible, but it is important to keep in mind that such high returns also carry higher risks. Here are some tips to maximize returns and manage risks when investing in stock ETFs:

1. Conduct thorough research: Before investing in a stock ETF, it is important to conduct detailed research on the companies included in the benchmark index and the market sectors covered by the ETF. This way, it will be possible to identify growth opportunities and avoid high-risk companies or sectors.

2. Diversification: Diversification is essential to reduce investment risk. Investing in different stock ETFs covering various sectors and markets can help spread risk and achieve more stable returns over time.

3. Constant monitoring: It is important to constantly monitor the performance of the stock ETFs in which you have invested and

adjust your investment strategy based on market conditions. This way, you can seize earning opportunities and minimize loss risks.

4. In case of losses, it is advisable to wait if there are no urgent needs before selling. Over time, stock ETFs have always shown gains, recovering losses.

Possible risks in investing in stock ETFs

Although stock ETFs offer several advantages, it is important to keep in mind that there are also risks to consider during investment. Here are some of the main risks associated with stock ETFs:

1. Market risk: Stock ETFs are subject to market risk, namely the possibility that the value of the benchmark index on which they are based may decrease due to macroeconomic, political, or market factors.

2. Sector risk: Stock ETFs that replicate the performance of a single sector or industry are exposed to sector risk. If the sector in question experiences a decline, the stock ETF that replicates it may suffer significant losses.

3. Liquidity risk: Stock ETFs that invest in stocks of companies with low liquidity may be subject to liquidity risk, meaning the difficulty of buying or selling stocks at the desired price.

4. Currency risk: Stock ETFs investing in foreign markets are exposed to currency risk, meaning that fluctuations in the exchange rate between currencies may negatively affect investment returns.

By taking these risks into account and adopting a prudent investment strategy, it is possible to achieve attractive returns by investing in stock ETFs and exceed 20% per year. However, it is important to remember that past returns do not guarantee future returns and it is always advisable to consult a financial advisor before making significant investment decisions.

24. Market Risks of ETFs

Stock ETFs are an increasingly popular investment tool among investors, thanks to their diversified and transparent nature. For those looking to achieve attractive returns while also reducing investment risk, stock ETFs represent a very interesting option.

But what are the possibilities of earning by investing in stock ETFs and how is it possible to achieve a return of over 20% per year? In this article, we will explore the potentials and risks of investing in stock ETFs and provide useful tips to maximize returns.

Why invest in stock ETFs?

Stock ETFs represent an effective way to invest in stocks of different companies, reducing the risk of concentration and improving portfolio diversification. Thanks to the presence of a basket of stocks within a single instrument, ETFs offer investors the opportunity to participate in the potential appreciation of the stock market as a whole, without having to choose and monitor individual stocks.

Moreover, stock ETFs offer low management costs compared to mutual funds and investment trusts, making them a cost-effective choice for investors looking to maximize net returns.

How to achieve a return of over 20% per year?

For example, many ETFs that invest in the S&P 500 (the best US companies) and global MSCI World stocks may have returns exceeding 20%.

Achieving a return of over 20% per year by investing in stock ETFs may be possible, but it is important to keep in mind that such high returns also come with higher risks. Here are some tips to maximize returns and manage risks when investing in stock ETFs:

1. Conduct thorough research: Before investing in a stock ETF, it is important to conduct detailed research on the companies included in the benchmark index and the market sectors that the ETF covers. This way, it will be possible to identify growth opportunities and avoid high-risk companies or sectors.

2. Diversification: Diversification is essential to reduce investment risk. Investing in different stock ETFs that cover various sectors and markets can help spread risk and achieve more stable returns over time.

3. Constant monitoring: It is important to constantly monitor the performance of the stock ETFs in which you have invested and adjust your investment strategy based on market conditions. This way, you can seize

earning opportunities and minimize the risks of loss.

4. Where losses occur, it is advisable to wait if there are no pressing needs before selling. Over time, stock ETFs have always recorded gains, recovering losses.

Potential risks of investing in stock ETFs

Although stock ETFs offer several advantages, it is important to keep in mind that there are also risks to consider during investment. Here are some of the main risks associated with stock ETFs:

1. Market risk: Stock ETFs are subject to market risk, namely the possibility that the value of the benchmark index on which they are based may decrease due to macroeconomic, political, or market factors.

2. Sectoral risk: Stock ETFs that replicate the performance of a single sector or industry are exposed to sectoral risk. If the sector in question experiences a decline, the stock ETF that replicates it could incur significant losses.

3. Liquidity risk: Stock ETFs that invest in stocks of companies with low liquidity are subject to liquidity risk, making it difficult to buy or sell shares at the desired price.

4. Currency risk: Stock ETFs that invest in foreign markets are exposed to currency risk, namely the possibility that exchange rate fluctuations between currencies may negatively affect the investment return.

Taking these risks into account and adopting a prudent investment strategy, it is possible to achieve attractive returns by investing in stock ETFs and exceed 20% per year. However, it is important to remember that past returns do not guarantee future returns and it is always advisable to consult a financial advisor before making significant investment decisions.

25.ETF Liquidity Risks

Exchange Traded Funds (ETFs) are an increasingly popular investment tool among investors, as they offer a range of benefits such as portfolio diversification and ease of trading on the stock exchange. However, like any form of investment, ETFs are subject to various risks, including liquidity risk.

Liquidity risk refers to an investor's ability to buy or sell a share of an ETF without significantly impacting the market price. In other words, a liquid ETF is a tool that can be easily and quickly traded without experiencing a significant impact on the prices of the underlying stocks.

Liquid ETFs have a high trading volume on the market and a wide spread between the buying price and the selling price. Conversely, illiquid ETFs have a lower trading volume and a narrower spread, meaning it can be difficult to buy or sell them without incurring significant losses.

Liquidity risk can be particularly problematic during market instability or extraordinary events that lead to increased volatility. In these situations, investors may find it difficult to sell their ETF shares at the desired price, or even sell them at all.

The main causes of ETF illiquidity include the presence of thinly traded or hard-to-liquidate underlying securities, high market volatility, the presence of closed markets or those subject to temporary restrictions, and the use of complex derivative instruments.

One of the main criticisms leveled at ETFs concerns the exponential growth of the sector in recent years, which has led to the creation of increasingly specialized funds focused on specific market sectors. These funds may be more susceptible to liquidity risk, as they may have a more limited investor base and lower liquidity compared to more traditional funds.

To mitigate ETF liquidity risk, investors can adopt various strategies. Firstly, it is important to pay attention to the size and trading volume of the ETF in which you intend to invest. ETFs with high trading volume and a broad investor base are generally considered less susceptible to liquidity risk.

Furthermore, it is advisable to diversify your ETF portfolio by investing in asset allocation tools that cover a wide range of markets and sectors. This way, investors can reduce the risk of concentration in a single fund and increase the overall liquidity of their portfolio.

European ETF regulations also require fund managers to ensure the liquidity of the underlying securities by creating and redeeming ETF shares directly with the issuer. This mechanism, known as the creation/redemption mechanism, helps maintain an adequate level of fund liquidity and limit risk for investors.

It should be noted that, despite the liquidity risk of ETFs, these instruments still remain an effective and convenient way to diversify an investment portfolio and gain exposure to a wide range of markets and sectors. Investors can reduce liquidity risk through proper portfolio management and careful selection of investment tools.

The liquidity risk of ETFs is an aspect to consider for investors looking to use these financial instruments. With the right attention and precautions, it is possible to mitigate this risk and benefit from the investment opportunities offered by ETFs.

26. ETF Management Risks

Exchange-traded funds (ETFs) have become increasingly popular among investors in recent years. These instruments offer a number of advantages over traditional mutual funds, including greater liquidity and diversification as well as lower fees. However, like any type of investment, ETFs also come with management risks that investors should be aware of before deciding whether to include them in their portfolio.

One of the main risks associated with ETFs is the possibility of suffering financial losses due to market volatility. ETFs are comprised of a collection of securities, such as stocks, bonds, or commodities, that track a specific index. If the market in which these securities are contained experiences a significant fluctuation, the ETF may incur losses. This risk is particularly evident in periods of economic or political instability, when markets tend to fluctuate more frequently.

Another risk to consider is related to the structure of the ETFs themselves. ETFs are traded on exchanges like stocks, which means their price can fluctuate throughout the day based on supply and demand. This difference between the net asset value (NAV) and the market price can create arbitrage opportunities for traders, but it can also pose risks for investors who do not take these fluctuations into account.

Additionally, ETFs can be exposed to counterparty risks as they often use financial derivatives to replicate the performance of an underlying index. If the counterparty with whom the ETF has entered into the derivative contract fails to meet its financial obligations, the ETF may incur significant losses. This risk is amplified in cases where the ETF relies on complex derivatives, such as credit default swaps, which carry a high credit risk.

Another factor to consider is the liquidity risk of ETFs. Although ETFs are generally more liquid than mutual funds, there are situations where market liquidity could be compromised. For example, in periods of high market volatility or during a global financial crisis, the demand and supply of ETFs may not be aligned, causing a discrepancy between the market price and the intrinsic value of the ETF.

Lastly, there is the management risk associated with the ETF's structure itself. ETFs are managed by management companies that are tasked with replicating the performance of the benchmark index on which they are based. If the management of the ETF is not effective in tracking the index's performance, investors may suffer losses. Additionally, management decisions made by the company may not align with the investors' objectives, causing further issues.

ETFs offer investors many opportunities for diversification and liquidity, but they also come with management risks that should be taken into consideration. It is important for investors to be aware of these risks and carefully evaluate whether ETFs are suitable for their investment needs before making a decision. Consulting with a professional financial advisor can be a great way to get a comprehensive analysis of the risks associated with ETFs and to develop an appropriate investment strategy.

27. Risks of Financial Leverage

Financial leverage is a concept that involves using borrowed funds to increase the potential return of an investment. ETFs that use financial leverage seek to provide a higher return than the benchmark index they track, using debt to amplify the movements of financial markets.

While financial leverage can increase potential profits, it also increases risks. ETFs that use financial leverage are more sensitive to market fluctuations and may incur greater losses compared to traditional ETFs. Additionally, financial leverage increases interest costs and may make it more difficult for the ETF to maintain a consistent leverage ratio over time.

Another risk associated with ETFs with financial leverage is counterparty risk. Since these ETFs use financial derivatives to achieve leverage, there is a risk that the counterparty with whom the ETF has entered into a contract may not be able to fulfill its obligations. This can lead to significant losses for ETF investors.

Furthermore, ETFs with financial leverage are more complex than traditional ETFs and may be more difficult to evaluate. Investors must have a deeper understanding of financial markets and derivative products to fully grasp how these instruments work and what risks they entail.

It is important to emphasize that financial leverage is not for all investors. Investors who do not fully understand the risks associated with financial leverage or who are not willing to bear significant losses should probably avoid investing in ETFs with financial leverage.

To mitigate the risks associated with ETFs

with financial leverage, investors should adopt a long-term investment strategy and take into account their risk tolerance. Diversifying the portfolio is essential to reduce exposure to a single investment or asset class and protect capital from unforeseen market events.

Finally, investors should pay attention to the costs associated with ETFs with financial leverage. Since these ETFs are more complex and require more careful management, management costs may be higher compared to traditional ETFs. It is important to carefully evaluate these costs and ensure they are appropriate compared to the potential return on investment.

In conclusion, ETFs with financial leverage offer investors the opportunity to benefit from high potential returns, but they also entail significant risks. Before investing in ETFs with financial leverage, investors should carefully assess the risks and consider whether this type of investment is suitable for their risk profile and investment objectives. Planning and careful evaluation can help investors successfully navigate this complex sector and adopt an investment strategy that aligns with their long-term financial needs.

28. ETF Emission Risks

Liquidity risk. ETFs are traded on exchanges like stocks, and the liquidity of an ETF depends on the liquidity of the underlying securities. If the underlying securities are illiquid or if the market is volatile, investors may have difficulty selling their ETFs at the desired price.

To mitigate this risk, investors should pay attention to the liquidity of the underlying securities of the ETF they are investing in. Additionally, they should avoid trading ETFs during times of high volatility or in illiquid markets.

Tracking error risks

Another common risk associated with ETFs is tracking error risk. Tracking error occurs when the ETF does not accurately replicate the performance of its underlying index due to expenses, fees, or management errors. This can lead investors to receive lower returns compared to the benchmark index.

To mitigate this risk, investors should pay attention to the expenses and fees of the ETF they are investing in. Additionally, they should ensure that the ETF accurately tracks the performance of its underlying index by regularly checking the tracking error.

Credit spread risks

Another risk that investors should consider is credit spread risk. Credit spread refers to the difference between the interest rates on bonds issued by the ETF issuer and the yields on the underlying securities. If the credit of the ETF issuer deteriorates or if the interest rates on the bonds issued by the issuer increase, the value of the ETF may decrease.

To mitigate this risk, investors should pay

attention to the credit quality of the ETF issuer and the market conditions in which they operate. They should avoid investing in ETFs issued by entities with low credit ratings or in ETFs with high interest rates.

One of the main risks associated with ETFs is market risk. ETFs are composed of a basket of securities or other financial instruments, and their value is tied to the performance of these underlying securities. If the market experiences a correction or a crash, ETFs that track these markets will experience a loss in value.

To mitigate this risk, investors should diversify their portfolio by investing in ETFs that track different markets and sectors. This way, even if one sector experiences a correction, investors can reduce their losses by investing in more resilient sectors.

ETFs offer investors a convenient way to

diversify their portfolio and gain exposure to different markets and sectors. However, like all investments, ETFs come with risks that investors should consider before investing in them. With a proper assessment of risks and adequate diversification, investors can mitigate ETF emission risks and achieve more consistent returns in the long run.

29. Growth of the ETF sector

In recent years, the ETF sector has seen exponential growth, with the introduction of new innovative products that cater to market trends.

One of the most interesting sectors that has seen significant growth in the world of ETFs is artificial intelligence (AI). Artificial intelligence has become increasingly important in various industries, from automating business processes to autonomous vehicle technology. Investors are increasingly interested in investing in companies developing innovative AI-based solutions, and ETFs that follow this sector are attracting a growing number of investors.

New ETFs that track the AI sector offer investors the opportunity to participate in the growth of this revolutionary technology without having to select individual stocks.

These ETFs invest in companies that are leaders in the AI sector, from technology companies to industrial automation companies. Investors can benefit from the growth of this sector without having to conduct detailed research on individual companies.

Another sector that is attracting more interest among investors is cryptocurrencies. Cryptocurrencies have become increasingly popular due to their decentralized technology and growing acceptance as a means of payment. Investors interested in participating in the growth of cryptocurrencies can now do so through specific ETFs that track this sector.

ETFs that track the cryptocurrency sector invest in a range of popular cryptocurrencies such as Bitcoin and Ethereum, offering investors diversified exposure to this high-potential growth sector. These ETFs closely monitor the cryptocurrency market and offer investors a simple solution to invest in this sector without having to directly manage cryptocurrencies.

The growth of the ETF sector and the introduction of new products such as AI and cryptocurrency ETFs are great news for investors looking to diversify their portfolios and benefit from the potential growth opportunities offered by these innovative sectors. ETFs offer investors a simple and efficient solution to invest diversely and target specific technology and innovation sectors.

The growth of the ETF sector and the introduction of new products such as AI and cryptocurrency ETFs offer investors a wide range of opportunities to diversify their portfolios and benefit from market trends. ETFs represent an efficient and accessible way to invest in high-growth sectors, offering investors the opportunity to participate in the growth of these innovative technologies without having to manage individual stocks or cryptocurrencies.

30.Creating a Balanced Portfolio with ETFs

Exchange-Traded Funds, also known by the acronym ETF, are gaining popularity among investors due to their variety, transparency, and low costs. ETFs are investment funds that replicate the performance of an index or a basket of stocks, bonds, or commodities. They can be traded on the stock exchange like stocks, offering investors the opportunity to diversify their portfolio in a simple and efficient way.

One of the main advantages of ETFs is that they allow investors to obtain diversified and balanced exposure without the need to purchase individual stocks or bonds. Furthermore, ETFs are managed passively, which means that investors do not have to worry about making active investment choices, but can benefit from the overall market performance.

Creating a balanced portfolio with ETFs is an excellent strategy for those looking to achieve effective diversification and mitigate investment risk. In this article, we will explore how to build a balanced portfolio with ETFs, taking into account the different asset categories and the investor's investment objective.

1. Define investment objectives

Before starting to build a portfolio with ETFs, it is important to clearly define investment objectives. For example, an investor may be interested in achieving long-term income for retirement, or may be looking for current income to supplement their income source. Others may have more aggressive goals, such as seeking high short-term returns.

Once investment objectives are defined, suitable ETFs that meet these objectives can be selected. For example, if you want to generate current income, you may consider purchasing ETFs that replicate high dividend stock indices. If you are looking for long-term returns, you may consider ETFs that replicate global stock indices.

2. Define the asset proportion in your allocation

Once investment objectives are defined, it is important to determine the proportion of assets to allocate in each category. A balanced portfolio usually includes a combination of stocks, bonds, and other asset classes such as commodities or real estate. The proportion of assets will depend on the risks and preferences of the investor, as well as their risk tolerance.

For example, a young investor with a high risk tolerance may opt for greater exposure to stocks, while an older investor may prefer greater exposure to bonds to reduce overall portfolio risk. It is essential to find a balance between risk and expected returns based on investment objectives.

3. Select the most suitable ETFs for each asset category

Once the proportion of assets to be allocated in the portfolio is defined, it is possible to select the most suitable ETFs for each asset category. There are numerous ETFs that cover a wide range of stock, bond, and commodity indices. It is important to pay attention to the quality and liquidity of selected ETFs, as well as to management costs and ETF transparency.

For example, if you want exposure to global stocks, you may consider purchasing ETFs that replicate indices such as the S&P 500 or the MSCI World. If you are looking for exposure to bonds, you may consider ETFs that replicate short, medium, or long-term bond indices.

4. Monitor and rebalance the portfolio over time

Once you have built your balanced portfolio with ETFs, it is important to regularly monitor the performance of ETFs and rebalance the portfolio based on financial market fluctuations and investor investment objectives. For example, if global stocks are experiencing a sharp correction, it may be time to realign the portfolio by reducing exposure to stocks and increasing exposure to bonds.

It is also important to consider the management costs of ETFs and periodically evaluate whether the selected ETFs are still in line with the investor's investment strategy. If necessary, you can replace ETFs with more suitable ones or ones with better performance.

Creating a balanced portfolio with ETFs is an excellent strategy for effective diversification and mitigating investment risk. It is important to clearly define investment objectives, determine the proportion of assets to allocate, select the most suitable ETFs, and monitor and rebalance the portfolio over time. With the right strategy and proper management, ETFs can be an effective tool for achieving long-term financial goals.

31.How to make an accumulation plan in ETF

An ETF accumulation plan is an investment method that allows savers to invest regularly in Exchange Traded Funds (ETFs) in an automated way. This method is particularly suitable for those who wish to build a diversified portfolio over time, without having to make investments in a single solution. In this article, we will explore how to make an ETF accumulation plan and outline the necessary steps to get started.

What is an ETF and why invest in it

An Exchange-Traded Fund (ETF) is an investment fund that tracks the performance of an index or a basket of assets. ETFs are traded like stocks on the stock exchange and can be bought and sold during market trading hours. ETFs offer great diversification because they invest in a variety of financial assets, such as stocks, bonds, commodities, or real estate.

Investing in ETFs offers several advantages over other types of investments. First of all, ETFs have lower management costs compared to traditional mutual funds. Additionally, ETFs are highly liquid, meaning they can be easily bought and sold on financial markets. Finally, ETFs offer great diversification because they allow you to invest in a broad market or sector with a single transaction.

Why make an ETF accumulation plan

Making an ETF accumulation plan can be a great way to build a diversified portfolio over time. This investment method allows you to invest a fixed amount regularly in ETFs through automatic debit to your current account. This way, you can benefit from the cost averaging strategy, which means investing consistently regardless of market fluctuations.

Furthermore, with an ETF accumulation plan, you can gradually expose yourself to financial markets, reducing the risk of making wrong investments in a single solution. Finally, an ETF accumulation plan is a simple and convenient method to invest in the long term without having to constantly monitor the market.

How to make an ETF accumulation plan

To make an ETF accumulation plan, you need to follow some fundamental steps. Here is a detailed guide on how to get started:

1. Define investment objectives

The first step in making an ETF accumulation plan is to define your investment objectives. It is important to decide how much you want to invest, for how long, and for what purpose. For example, you can decide to invest a fixed amount every month for a period of 10 years to achieve long-term returns.

2. Choose suitable ETFs

Once you have defined your investment objectives, you need to choose ETFs that are suitable for your risk profile and investment goals. It is advisable to diversify your portfolio by investing in ETFs that cover different sectors and markets. You can consult a financial advisor for advice on which ETFs to choose.

3. Open a deposit account

To make an ETF accumulation plan, you need to open a deposit account with a bank or an online broker. This account will automatically debit the amounts intended for investment in

ETFs. It is important to check the fees charged by the deposit account and make sure to choose a cost-effective account.

4. Schedule the automatic purchase of ETFs, for example, spend 100 every month on one or more chosen ETF funds

Once you have opened the deposit account, you can schedule the automatic purchase of ETFs. This can be done by choosing the amount to invest and the frequency of purchases (e.g., monthly or quarterly). This way, the amounts intended for investment will be automatically debited from the current account and invested in the selected ETFs.

5. Monitor and update the ETF accumulation plan

Once the ETF accumulation plan has started, it is important to regularly monitor the performance of investments and update the plan according to your needs and goals. It is advisable to consult a financial advisor to evaluate the effectiveness of the plan and make any changes based on market conditions.

Making an ETF accumulation plan is a great way to invest in the long term in a simple and convenient way. By following the steps described in this article, you can build a diversified portfolio over time and benefit from the growth of financial markets. Consulting a financial advisor can be helpful to get personalized advice and optimize your ETF accumulation plan.

32. The ETC

Exchange Traded Commodities (ETCs) are a type of financial instrument that allows investors to gain exposure to commodities such as gold, silver, oil, and agricultural products through tradable securities. ETCs are similar to exchange-traded funds (ETFs) in that they are listed on stock exchanges and can be bought and sold throughout the trading day.

Unlike ETFs, which typically track an index or a basket of stocks, ETCs are designed to track the price of a commodity or a group of commodities. This means that investors can access the commodity markets without having to own the physical asset itself. ETCs are particularly popular among investors who want to diversify their portfolios and hedge against inflation or economic uncertainty.

There are several ways in which investors can gain exposure to commodities through ETCs. One common method is through physically backed ETCs, which hold the actual physical commodity in storage. For example, a physically backed gold ETC would hold gold bars in a secure vault. This allows investors to benefit from the price movements of the underlying commodity without having to worry about storage or maintenance costs.

Another type of ETC is synthetic ETCs, which use derivatives such as swaps and futures contracts to track the price of the commodity. These ETCs are often used when it is not practical to physically store the commodity, such as with oil or agricultural products. While synthetic ETCs can be more complex and carry additional risks, they can also offer higher levels of liquidity and flexibility.

Investing in ETCs can provide a range of benefits for investors. For one, ETCs offer easy access to commodity markets without the need for specialized knowledge or expertise. They also provide diversification benefits, as commodities tend to have low correlation with traditional asset classes like stocks and bonds. This can help reduce overall portfolio risk and increase returns over the long term.

Furthermore, investing in ETCs can be a cost-effective way to gain exposure to commodities. ETCs typically have lower management fees and expenses compared to actively managed commodity funds, making them an attractive option for investors looking to minimize costs. Additionally, ETCs are traded on stock exchanges, which means that investors can buy and sell them quickly and easily, just like stocks or ETFs.

Despite their many benefits, ETCs come with their own set of risks that investors should be aware of. Commodity prices can be highly volatile and subject to external factors such as geopolitical events, weather conditions, and supply and demand dynamics. This can lead to sharp price fluctuations in ETCs, which can result in significant losses for investors.

Additionally, since ETCs are traded on stock exchanges, they are also subject to market risks, such as liquidity risk and tracking error. Liquidity risk refers to the possibility that there may not be enough buyers or sellers for a particular ETC, which can result in wider bid-ask spreads and lower trading volumes. Tracking error, on the other hand, refers to the discrepancy between the performance of the ETC and the underlying commodity it is tracking.

Exchange Traded Commodities offer investors a convenient and cost-effective way to gain exposure to commodity markets. They provide diversification benefits, easy access, and potentially lower costs compared to other investment vehicles. However, investors should be aware of the risks associated with ETCs, including commodity price volatility, market risks, and tracking error. As with any investment, it is important to carefully consider your investment goals and risk tolerance before investing in ETCs.

Index